HOW TO

GET A JOB

USING AI

Job Search Smarter, not Harder, using Artificial Intelligence

Sandra Ramsay-Nicol

For more information about the author and further materials:

Email: booksbysandrarn@gmail.com

Cover design: Janika

ISBN: 978-36917-4389-0

DEDICATION

To my husband, Syble and our children, Renee, Triniti and EJ

I love you more than words can express.

To my mum, Gloria Alex-Eyitene

Your enduring love and prayers are my anchor. I love you!

To my mother-in-law, Princess Nicol

Always there for us…loving you is easy.

To my siblings, Kwame, Ian, Carol, Tony, Laura and Ogaga

Daddy's legacy lives on through all of us. I hold you dear.

To my editors, Rachel and the Heritage Publishers.

Your commitment to this book made it possible.

To God,

I am profoundly grateful.

How to Get a Job Using AI

TABLE OF CONTENTS

ABOUT THE AUTHOR

Sandra Ramsay-Nicol is a seasoned entrepreneur with a remarkable professional journey. Unlike conventional business leaders, Sandra stands out as a serial entrepreneur, bringing a wealth of experience and innovation to each venture.

Commencing her career as an Accountant, Sandra's proficiency extended beyond number-crunching, revealing a deep-seated passion for technology. From setting up cutting-edge accounting systems to serving as a Software Training Consultant at Sage plc, Sandra navigated the tech landscape with a distinctive touch.

Sandra's entrepreneurial spirit didn't stop at calculations and software; she developed a bespoke examination feedback software that has positively impacted thousands across the UK.

Sandra emerges as a fervent advocate for Artificial Intelligence (AI) adoption. As a trailblazer in the realm of silicon superheroes, she not only champions AI but actively participates in speaking engagements on the subject. Sandra's commitment goes beyond words; she seamlessly integrates AI principles into her endeavours, presenting a holistic approach that combines expertise with advocacy.

Beyond the business realm, Sandra is an avid reader and a keen traveller, exploring the world with unbridled curiosity. While her business acumen is evident, Sandra holds a profound appreciation for her Christian faith activities and cherishes moments with her family.

Sandra Ramsay-Nicol is a tech-savvy serial entrepreneur, who is passionate about of all things AI. She is also the author of **"*Smart Mums Don't Ignore AI*."** To contact Sandra for speaking engagements or AI consultancy, **email**: **booksbysandrarn@gmail.com**

CHAPTER 1

THE CURRENT UK LABOUR MARKET

"Where challenges meet opportunities, and your next career chapter awaits."

The Current UK Labour Market

Before we delve into the essence of this book, let's take a moment to look at what's happening in the UK job market right now. A recent survey by Indeed Hiring Lab in 2023 found that recruiters are advertising fewer job vacancies. This means that job seekers might not feel as confident about finding a new job quickly. It is important to understand these changes and how they might impact your job search journey.

The graph below shows the drop in confidence levels from 46% in early 2022 to 39% in the first quarter of 2023.

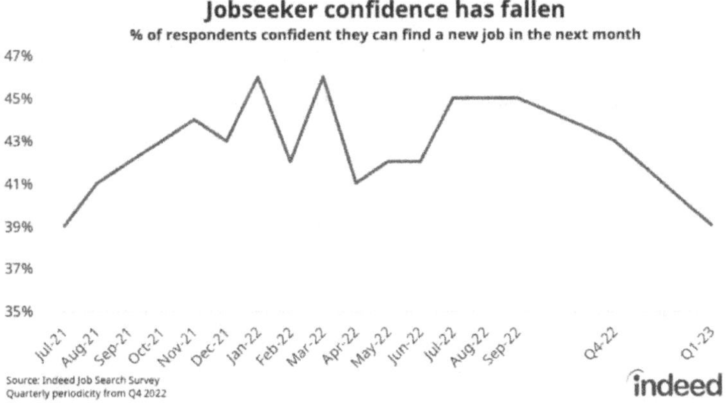

Line chart showing the percentage of respondents to Indeed's job search survey who are confident of finding a new job in the next month. Optimism fell in March to its lowest level since the survey began in July 2021.

In the last few years, right after the tough times of the 2020 pandemic, there was a shortage of workers. The demand for workers was higher than the number of people available to work, but things are starting to shift. Why? Well, there are a few reasons, but one of them is that many students who chose to stay in school longer because of the pandemic, have now joined to the workforce.

Secondly, there are fewer people of working age, actively looking for work.

Finally, with many people working from home, there are fewer people actually out and about in towns and cities. For example, in the city of London this has affected the demand for in-person services (like bars, café, restaurants) professional occupations (gyms, beauty) and distribution services (couriers, deliveries). When the demand for services goes down, employers stop hiring, which in turn means there are fewer job postings. It's like a ripple effect.

The Current Position

At the time of writing, there are 1.2 jobseekers for each vacancy, (i.e. the number of unemployed people for each vacancy). After the pandemic in 2022, this peaked to about 4.5 people per vacancy. The research suggests that this may be because employers are prioritising retaining and retraining existing workers rather than hiring new ones. There are still vacancies posted but they vary by occupation.

Let's look at the table below which shows sectors with the highest and lowest job postings or vacancies.

Occupational job posting trends vary widely

Occupation	Indeed Job Postings Index, 1 Feb 2020 = 100, to 12 May 2023
Strongest performers	
Social Science	206
Aviation	203
Physicians & Surgeons	194
Therapy	193
Community & Social Service	192
Medical Technicians	180
Weakest performers	
Beauty & Wellness	84
Information Design & Documentation	84
Media & Communications	78
Software Development	78
Legal	75
Mathematics	67

Source: Indeed. Data seasonally adjusted.

indeed

Table showing the strongest and weakest job postings trends by occupation. Social science job postings are furthest above pre-pandemic levels, while mathematics postings are furthest below the baseline.

You will notice that the sectors with a drop in job postings are typically those that can be carried out by technology. Services like Beauty and Wellness have been affected by people working from home and inflation in the economy.

The good news is that the adoption of AI has created new jobs for which there is a shortage of skilled personnel. Jobs like machine learning specialists, prompt engineers, data engineers, data analysts etc, continue to see an increase in job postings. With the decrease in overall job postings and stiffer competition in getting a job, you must give yourself the competitive edge by turning to AI tools to help you write more compelling job applications.

I was surprised to read that in an interview with Teaching Matters, a University of Edinburgh lecturer stated that *"there had been a 'decline in applicants making use of ChatGPT', due to a lack of understanding as to how to create good outputs from the inputs that they chose: what is known in information technology as 'garbage in, garbage out'.*

It is, therefore, very important that you understand how these tools work and how to use them; as such, we will explore this in the next few chapters.

DO YOU KNOW THAT....

*The most challenging issue
recruiters face is finding
quality candidates.*

CHAPTER 2

HOW AI IS USED IN THE JOB SEARCH PROCESS

"The job search isn't just a process, it's your pathway to possibilities."

How AI is used in the Job Search Process

In this book, I will show how you can make Artificial Intelligence (AI) work for you in finding a job. It's like having a helpful assistant that makes your job search process easier, finding the relevant opportunities and making you stand out as the perfect candidate for the job you desire. Let's look at how AI can be a game changer in the job market. We'll go into more detail about each of these areas in the chapters ahead.

1. AI for CV Writing Assistance

CVs (Curriculum Vitae) are often the first "go-to place" when employers are searching for prospective employees. Increasingly, employers are now using AI tools like Applicant Tracking Systems (ATS) to go through these CVs. These systems use keywords to sort and rank job applications received. As someone looking for a job, you can use AI tools to make your CV even better by finding and including the right keywords. This way, you have a better chance of getting through the ATS screening. We will look at keywords in the upcoming chapters.

2. AI for Matching Candidates and Jobs

Do you know that many job portals are essentially search engines for jobs? Platforms like LinkedIn and Indeed use AI algorithms to match job seekers with suitable positions. So, when you provide your work history, skills and preferences, these platforms can present you with job opportunities that align with your qualifications, thereby saving you valuable time and effort. I don't know about you, but I would be delighted to get any help I can to speed up my job applications.

3. AI for Cover Letter Revisions

Your first interaction with a potential employer often happens through a cover letter and believe me, it can either make or break your application. We all know how small mistakes, like grammar errors and typos, can lead to your application being rejected. But here's where the magic of AI tools comes in. By tapping into these smart tools, you not only get valuable insights but also get your cover letter polished and improved for the specific job you are applying to. So, do embrace the power of technology to ensure your applications stand out in the competitive job market.

4. AI for Interview Preparation

AI-powered interview preparation tools can simulate job interviews, offering feedback on your responses and body language. This helps you refine your interview skills and boost your confidence.

5. AI for Auto Filling of Job Applications

AI can be used to automatically complete job applications. The convenience of these autofill tools means that you avoid the tedious task of form-filling. It turns the job application process in to a smooth, efficient experience.

6. AI for Career Coaching

AI algorithms can give personalised career advice and even suggest ways to improve your job search strategy. They may recommend additional skills to acquire, certifications to obtain or even networking opportunities to explore. Isn't that awesome?

7. AI for Job Predictions

Do you know that some AI tools can provide insights into the likelihood of you landing a job at a particular company? How? Well, they look at historical data, the current state of the job market and individual qualifications to estimate your chances of success for a specific role. These are used by professionals in various industries. e.g. Googlecloud, AutoML, Tableau.

A word of caution though! While AI algorithms and tools can greatly enhance your job search, it's important to remember that they are tools to assist you, not replace you. You must still invest the effort in building a strong professional network and improving your interview skills. Remember, it is essential to remain cautious and ethical when using AI in your job search.

CHAPTER 3

HOW AI JOB ALGORITHMS WORK

---

*"Unlock possibilities,
One Algorithm at a time."*

AI Algorithms Explained

In today's digital world, finding a job is not just about handing in a CV. Now, super-smart computer rules, called algorithms, are like your job-search buddies. There is a strong relationship between job seeking and algorithms. They help suggest awesome jobs you might really like. This chapter is all about how these digital helpers are changing the way we find the perfect job and how employers use them. Let's explore how these computer pals are making job hunting easier and more exciting!"

My most fond memory of the word 'algorithm' was when I watched a Dragon's Den pitch in 2015, where a lady was pitching for funds to expand her platform "Intern Avenue," designed to assist graduates in finding internships. She referred to the 'algorithms' of the platform she had developed, and I remember thinking how intelligent she sounded, using such a technical term. I knew she'd get a Dragon on board because she sure sounded like she knew what she was talking about. Needless to say, she had the Dragons falling head over heels to fund her project. She later sold the company to Bright Network, for a tidy sum, I guess!

> **Bright Network acquires graduate hire-matching platform Intern Avenue**
>
> *Dupsy Abiola launched Intern Avenue in 2012, using technology to automate the process of selecting and sourcing candidates. It claims to be able to reduce time and expenses by up to 90%. Today, the platform helps more than 75,000 students and graduates to work with over 550 employers across the UK and Europe.*

So, I thought I'd start by explaining the word 'algorithm' in the easiest way I could think of.

'Algorithm' – what does this word mean?

An algorithm is the set of rules a machine (especially a computer) follows to achieve a particular goal. Just like when you follow a recipe to make your favourite meal, a computer follows an algorithm to perform a task.

Imagine you want to teach a robot to brush its teeth. The robot can't do it by itself, so you create a list of very specific steps.

- *First, it puts toothpaste on the toothbrush.*
- *Then, it moves the toothbrush to its mouth.*

- *Next, it brushes up and down for two minutes.*

- *Finally, it rinses its mouth with water.*

So, an algorithm is just a set of very clear instructions that tells a computer or a robot what to do, step by step. It helps them solve problems and complete tasks, just like following a recipe helps you make your favourite meal!

So, let's see what an algorithm design for both job hunters and employers would look like. You could create your own using templates available in www.edrawsoft.com or Microsoft Word.

A. EXAMPLE OF A JOB SEEKERS ALGORITHM

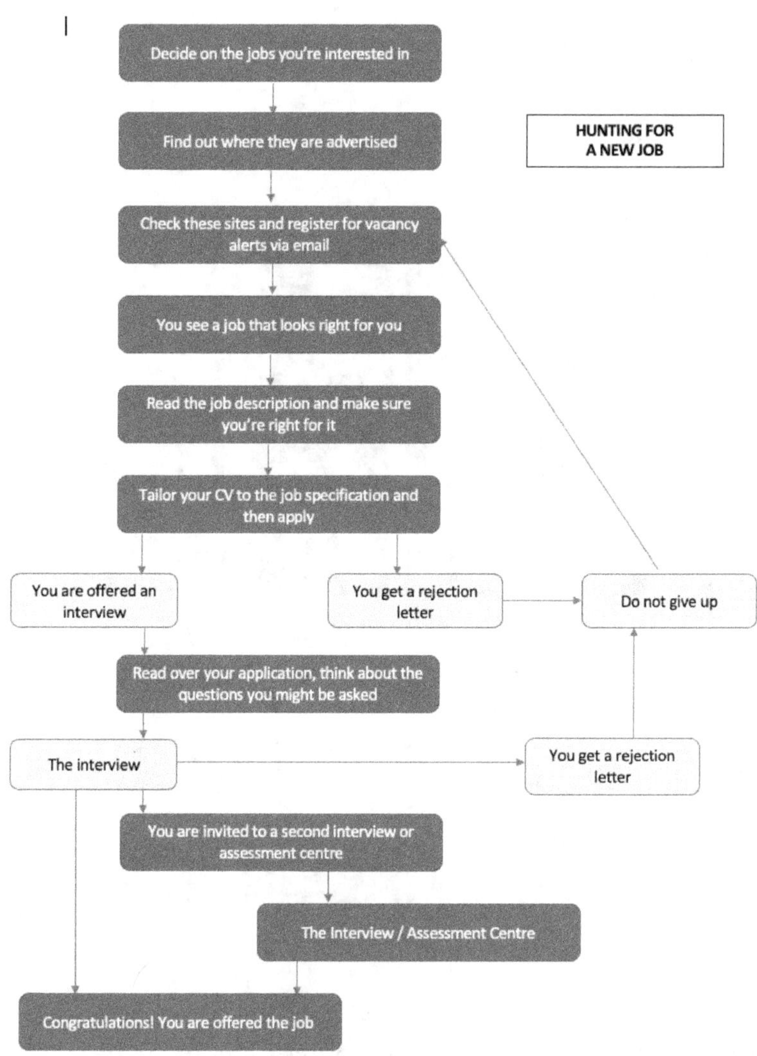

B. EXAMPLE OF AN EMPLOYER'S ALGORITHM

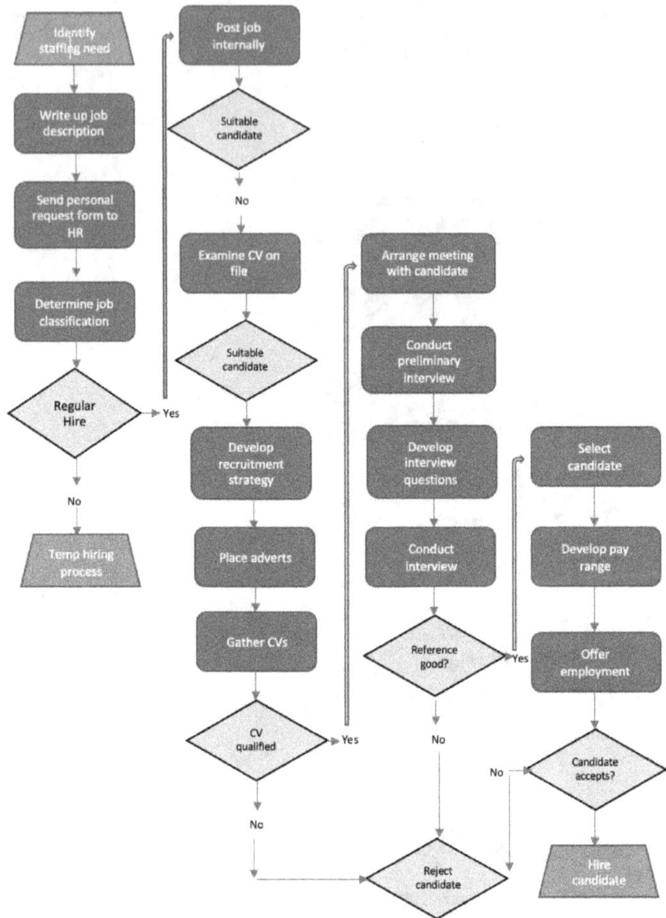

Free template courtesy of www.edrawsoft.com

CHAPTER 4

HOW TO DEVELOP A JOB SEARCH STRATEGY

*"In the realm of career pursuits,
patience is not just a virtue; it's a strategy."*

How to Develop a Job Search Strategy

Having a solid plan in place when you are hunting for a job is super important. Imagine you are setting off on a journey without a map – it can get confusing and take a lot longer to reach your destination. Similarly, without a job search plan, finding the right job can be overwhelming and less effective. So, having a plan is like having your own guide to navigate the competitive job market.

Let's take a closer look at Sarah, a pro in marketing who was eager for a change. She didn't just dive into job boards randomly; instead, she made a thoughtful plan. First, she figured out exactly what kind of job she was looking for and what skills she wanted to highlight. Then, she tweaked her CV to showcase her best stuff, making sure it stood out. But that's not all – Sarah also reached out to people in her industry, building a network that could open doors for her. This strategic approach didn't just land her some informational interviews; it even led to a referral for a position that was a perfect fit for her.

So, having a job search plan is like having a roadmap. It helps you identify your strengths, pinpoint the jobs that match your goals, and make a memorable impression. This way, you are not just randomly searching for any job – you are on a purposeful journey to find the job that is just right for you.

Steps to Creating a Job Search Strategy

Creating a job search strategy can significantly improve your chances of finding the right job. Here are some steps to guide you:

STEP 1 - Self-Assessment:

- Identify your skills, strengths, and weaknesses.

- Consider your interests, values, and what you enjoy doing.

- Define your career goals and what you're looking for in a job.

STEP 2 - Research Job Market Trends:

- Explore current trends and demands in your industry.

- Research the job market to understand which skills are in demand.

- Identify growing sectors and potential employers.

STEP 3 - Create a Target List

- Make a list of companies or organisations you would like to work for.

- Prioritise them based on your preferences and values.

- Research each company's culture, values, and job opportunities.

STEP 4 - Optimise Your CV and Online Presence:

- Tailor your CV to the specific jobs you're targeting.

- Update your LinkedIn profile with a professional photo and detailed information.

- Ensure your online presence reflects your skills and experiences.

STEP 5 - Networking:

- Build and expand your professional network both online and offline.

- Attend industry events, conferences, and networking mixers.

- Connect with professionals in your field on platforms like LinkedIn.

STEP 6 - Set Realistic Goals:

- Define achievable short-term and long-term goals.

- Break down larger goals into smaller, actionable steps.

- Establish a timeline for accomplishing each goal.

STEP 7 - Prepare a Compelling Elevator Pitch:

- Develop a concise and engaging introduction about yourself.

- Highlight your skills, experiences, and what you're looking for in a job.

- Practice delivering your pitch confidently.

STEP 8 - Apply Strategically:

- Focus on quality over quantity when applying for jobs.

- Tailor your application for each position to showcase your relevance.

- Follow the application instructions carefully.

STEP 9 - Stay Organised:

- Create a system to keep track of the jobs you've applied for.

- Note deadlines, contacts, and any follow-up actions.

- Stay organised to manage multiple applications effectively.

STEP 10 - Adapt and Learn:

- Be open to adjusting your strategy based on feedback and results.

- Learn from each application and interview experience.

- Continuously refine your approach as you progress in your job search.

Remember, to use AI tools in developing your job search strategy. We will look at how this is done in the chapters that follow. A job search strategy is a dynamic plan that can evolve over time. Regularly reassess and adjust your strategy based on your experiences and changing circumstances.

Your AI Assisted Job Search Process

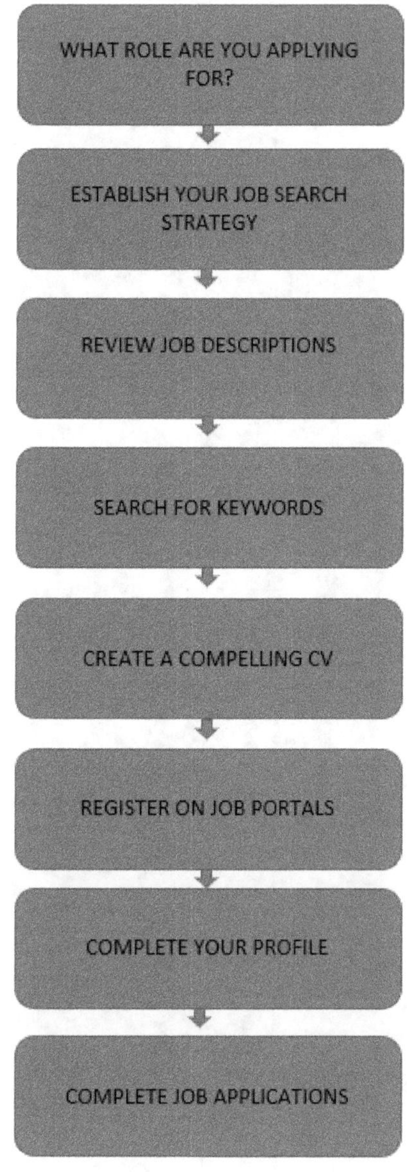

CHAPTER 5

THE IMPORTANCE OF KEYWORDS IN JOB HUNTING

"Keywords are the compass in the digital job market."

The Importance of Keywords in Job Hunting

Now let's look at the role keywords play in the job search process.

When looking at job applications and ATS (Applicant Tracking Systems) used by employers, keywords should be a critical part of your CV and job search strategy. "Why?" You may ask. I'll give a simple example which will explain the importance of keywords.

Let's imagine that every job posting is a puzzle, and your CV is that puzzle piece that needs to fit perfectly, to be considered for the job. The ATS is the sorting machine that helps the employer find the right puzzle pieces. This system is programmed to look for specific words and phrases which we call keywords in all CVs that it receives.

So how does it work?

When a company posts a job vacancy online, they include a list of requirements, qualifications and skills they are looking for in a candidate. These words and phrases are the keywords. They describe the 'puzzle piece' that is needed to fill that vacancy.

Below are examples of various job roles along with some keywords typically associated with each position. Make sure these keywords are prominently included in your CV, especially in the skills and experience sections. They are essential for optimising your CV and increasing your chances of passing through ATS screenings:

1. Software Engineer:

- **Keywords**: Java, Python, software development, agile, Git, problem-solving, algorithms, computer science, full-stack, software architecture.

2. Marketing Manager:

- **Keywords**: Marketing strategy, SEO, content marketing, social media, Google Analytics, branding, market research, campaign management, lead generation, email marketing.

3. Registered Nurse (RN):

- **Keywords**: Nursing, patient care, healthcare, CPR, critical care, electronic health records, nursing assessments, BLS certification, medical-surgical nursing.

4. Project Manager:

- **Keywords**: Project management, Agile methodology, PMP certification, budget management, stakeholder communication, risk assessment, project planning, resource allocation.

5. Data Analyst:

- **Keywords**: Data analysis, SQL, data visualization, Excel, statistical analysis, data mining, reporting, Python, Tableau, business intelligence.

6. Graphic Designer:

- **Keywords**: Graphic design, Adobe Creative Suite, branding, typography, visual communication, UI/UX design, Photoshop, InDesign, Illustrator.

7. Sales Representative:

- **Keywords**: Sales, lead generation, cold calling, CRM software, negotiation, relationship building, quota achievement, prospecting, customer service.

8. HR Manager:

- **Keywords**: Human resources, recruitment, employee relations, onboarding, performance management, HR policies, benefits administration, labour laws, HRIS.

9. Electrical Engineer:

- **Keywords**: Electrical engineering, circuit design, PCB layout, embedded systems, CAD software, troubleshooting, electronics, power distribution, control systems.

10. Content Writer:

- **Keywords**: Content writing, SEO, blogging, content marketing, copywriting, storytelling, grammar, editing, WordPress, keyword research.

11. Financial Analyst:

- **Keywords**: Financial analysis, budgeting, financial modelling, Excel, data analysis, investment analysis, finance, forecasting, financial reporting.

12. Mechanical Engineer:

- **Keywords**: Mechanical engineering, CAD, 3D modelling, thermodynamics, fluid dynamics, product design, mechanical systems, materials science.

These are just a few examples, and the specific keywords associated with a job may vary depending on the industry, company, and job description.

Other Keywords to Consider When Looking for a Job.

Keywords do not only relate to the position. For a more targeted approach for jobs that will be of great interest, consider using other keywords like:

1. **Job Titles**: Specific job titles like "Software Engineer," "Marketing Manager," "Registered Nurse," or "Project Manager."

2. **Skills**: Keywords related to your skills, such as "data analysis," "customer service," "project management," "web development," or "content writing."

3. **Location**: Keywords specifying the desired location, like "New York," "remote," "San Francisco," or "Europe."

4. **Industry or Field**: Keywords associated with the industry or field you're interested in, such as "healthcare," "finance," "technology," or "education."

5. **Experience Level**: Keywords like "entry-level," "senior," "internship," or "experienced" to indicate your experience level.

6. **Company Names**: Keywords related to specific companies you would like to work for.

7. **Job Type**: Keywords like "full-time," "part-time," "contract," or "freelance" to specify the type of job you're seeking.

8. **Qualifications**: Keywords connected to your qualifications, such as "Bachelor's degree," "PMP certification," or "nursing licence."

9. **Salary Range**: Keywords indicating the salary range or compensation expectations, like "competitive salary," "hourly wage," or "annual compensation."

> *When customising your CV for a particular job, it is important that you closely match the keywords from the job posting to maximise your chances of being selected for an interview.*

AI Tools for Keyword Checks

NAME	BRIEF INFORMATION	
Jobscan www.jobscan.co	Analyses how well your CV is tailored to a particular job.	
Kickresume www.kickresume.com	Grades your CV based on what recruiters look for. Gives it a score and shows a list of issues.	

Resume Worded www.resumeworded.com	Makes suggestions for improving keywords to match job descriptions.	
Postlander.com www.postlander.com	This will compare the keywords in your CV to what's included in the job description and will flag anything that is missing.	

CHAPTER 6

AI TOOLS FOR CV WRITING ASSISTANCE

"CV writing assistance is the guiding hand that transforms your professional journey into a compelling narrative."

AI for CV Writing Assistance

In this chapter, we'll explore how AI becomes your secret helper, making the task of creating a CV easier and more effective. As Michelle Obama wisely said, "Facing challenges isn't a setback; it's a chance to turn adversity into advantage." So, how can AI help you in writing your CV?

A. **Mastering Keywords with AI**: Your CV is like your professional introduction to employers, and AI is here to make it unforgettable. AI will help you find and use the right keywords for your industry, making your CV more visible and relevant. With AI precision, navigating the ever-changing job market becomes a breeze.

B. **AI Crafting Language and Content:** "Your words tell your story, and your story matters." Michelle Obama's wisdom echoes. AI will suggest powerful language, refine your achievements, and polish your content to showcase your skills and experiences.

C. **Tailoring Your CV:** With AI Personalisation CVs aren't one-size-fits-all. AI will tailor your CV based on industry trends and specific job needs. It will uncover the magic of personalisation, ensuring your CV aligns perfectly with what potential employers are looking for.

D. AI Feedback: For a flawless CV AI isn't just a tool; it's your CV coach. AI will provide constructive feedback, helping you perfect your CV. Whether it's improving formatting or enhancing overall impact, AI ensures your CV tells a polished story of your professional journey.

AI Tool for CV Writing

Here is a list of some AI powered CV creation tools you may wish to try.

NAME	BRIEF INFORMATION	
Grammarly.com www.grammarly.com	Has an AI powered Writing Assistant Free CV Builder.	
My Perfect CV www.myperfectcv.co.uk	Create your CV in minutes with many ready-made templates. Free sign up.	

Resumemaker.ai www.resumemaker.ai	Craft compelling career narratives with eye catching templates.	
Zety.ai www.zety.ai	Upload your own CV and Zety will generate the relevant information.	
Resume Worded www.resumeworded.com	Analyses your CV and gives you detailed feedback on how to improve..	

CV Improvement Prompts for Use in ChatGPT

An AI tool you could use to improve your CV is ChatGPT. Here are some ChatGPT prompts that can help you enhance your CV:

1. "I'd like to improve the structure and layout of my CV. Can you provide tips for creating a visually appealing and organised document?"

2. "What are the key sections that should be included in a CV, and how should they be ordered?"

3. "I want to make my CV stand out. Can you suggest creative ways to make it more memorable without being overly flashy?

4. "Can you provide advice on how to write a compelling professional summary or objective statement for my CV?"

5. "I'm considering a career change. How can I effectively highlight transferable skills and experiences in my CV?"

6. "What are some common CV mistakes to avoid, such as using jargon or overloading with information?"

7. "I'd like to tailor my CV for a specific job application. Can you provide guidance on customizing my CV to match a job description?"

8. "Can you help me write concise and impactful bullet points to describe my work experiences and achievements?"

9. "How can I emphasise my accomplishments and quantify my contributions in my CV to make it more compelling?"

10. "I have gaps in my work history. Can you suggest strategies for addressing these gaps in my CV?"

11. "I want to showcase my educational background effectively. Can you provide tips on how to format and detail my education section?"

12. "Can you help me identify relevant keywords and phrases to include in my CV for applicant tracking systems (ATS)?"

13. "What's the best way to list professional certifications, licenses, or additional qualifications on my CV?"

14. "I'm looking for guidance on writing an impressive 'Hobbies and Interests' section in my CV that can positively contribute to my image."

15. "Can you review my current CV and provide feedback or edits to improve its overall quality and effectiveness?"

These prompts can help you fine-tune your CV to better reflect your qualifications, skills, and experiences. A well-crafted CV is a powerful tool for making a positive impression on potential employers and securing job opportunities.

CV Improvement Personalised Prompts

When producing your CV is important to identify transferable skills. What skills have you developed or fine-tuned from your previous job that could be applied across various roles and industries?

Transferable Skills Prompts:

- Give me a list of transferable skills for a ______________ (your profession)

- Give me a list of top 5 transferable skills for a person transitioning from ___ to ___.

- How can I describe ________ skills on my CV?

To increase your chances of getting an interview, it is imperative that you tailor your CV to suit every job that you apply for. Use ChatGPT to give you keywords and phrases to help you stand out from the crowd.

Job Description Prompts:

- What keywords can I include in my CV for a _______ role?

- How can I tailor my CV for a _______ role?

- Align my CV with a job description for a ___________ role.

Bullet points on a CV are very powerful as the summarise your key achievements quickly and visibly. As such they need to be concise and create impact. ChatGPT can help you enhance these bullet points.

Enhance Bullet Points Prompts:

- What powerful verbs can I use to describe my leadership experience on my CV?

- Rewrite the bullet point – "Implemented a new booking system".

- Help me quantify my achievements in my last role.

Source: https://community.hros.io/transform-your-cv-with-ai-tools-boost-your-resume/

As we wrap up this chapter, remember that AI is your partner in self-presentation. With AI at your side, creating a standout CV becomes empowering and efficient. Let's embrace the age of AI-driven CVs, confident that our professional stories will not just be heard but will resonate strongly with potential employers. Your next career move is just a well-crafted CV away.

Should you wish to create a new CV from scratch using AI, follow these steps:

How to Create an AI CV Prompt from Scratch

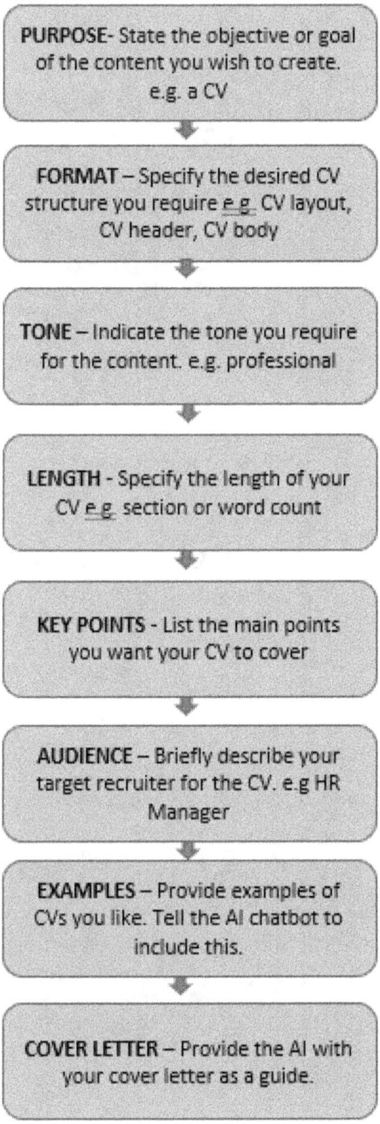

PURPOSE- State the objective or goal of the content you wish to create. e.g. a CV

FORMAT – Specify the desired CV structure you require e.g. CV layout, CV header, CV body

TONE – Indicate the tone you require for the content. e.g. professional

LENGTH - Specify the length of your CV e.g. section or word count

KEY POINTS - List the main points you want your CV to cover

AUDIENCE – Briefly describe your target recruiter for the CV. e.g HR Manager

EXAMPLES – Provide examples of CVs you like. Tell the AI chatbot to include this.

COVER LETTER – Provide the AI with your cover letter as a guide.

46

CHAPTER 7

AI TIPS FOR MATCHING CANDIDATES AND JOBS

"With the right algorithms, matching candidates to jobs is the magic that turns career dreams into reality."

How Do Recruiters Use AI for Matching Candidates and Jobs?

For employers and recruitment agencies hiring staff has always been labour intensive. They often have to sift through loads of irrelevant CVs and some pretty poor applications before they locate the right candidates who pass the initial screening stage.

Do you know that the average CV is only looked at for 10 seconds by employers?

The Artificial Intelligence (AI) revolution has created an opportunity for recruiters to save a considerable amount of time and resources by integrating AI tools in their selection process. Before we look at the AI tools used by employers, let's look at the methods employers use in hiring staff.

<u>Hiring methods used by recruiters.</u>

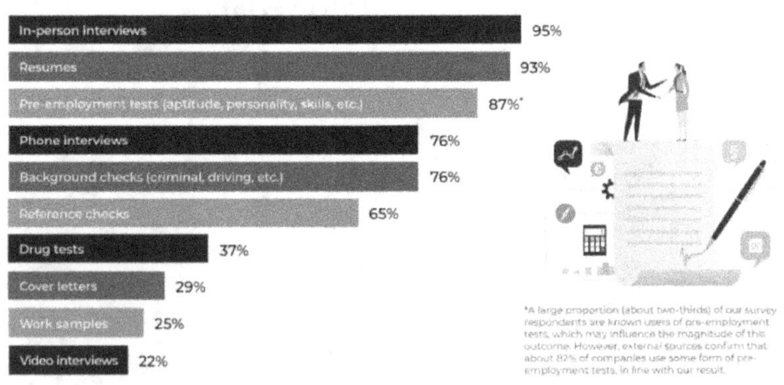

Source: Criteria Corp

The chart above clearly shows that the traditional methods of interviews and CVs (also known as resumes) are still the most commonly used hiring methods. I have included this chart here so that you can see the areas you need to focus on most when looking for a job. These are the areas that you could have an edge by taking advantage of the AI tools I discuss later on.

There are AI powered solutions that can help employers find the relevant candidates, contact them and even assess if they are the best fit for the organisation. These systems are often referred to as Applicant Tracking systems or ATS.

A. APPLICANT TRACKING SYSTEMS

An Applicant Tracking System (ATS) is a software application that is designed to help companies organise and automate the various tasks associated with hiring new employees. It is important for anyone looking for a job to understand these tools used by employers in order to increase their chance of passing through the initial ATS screening. So, let's delve further into understanding how ATS works.

1. **CV and Application Management**: When job seekers apply for a position, their CVs and applications are

typically submitted electronically. The ATS collects and stores this information in a structured format.

2. **Keyword Screening**: The ATS scans the submitted CVs and applications for specific keywords and phrases related to the job posting. It uses these keywords to filter and rank applicants based on their qualifications.

3. **Candidate Tracking**: The system tracks the progress of each candidate through the hiring process, from the initial application to the final hiring decision. This helps recruiters and hiring managers keep an organised system and ensures a consistent and fair process.

4. **Communication Management**: ATS software often includes communication tools to send automated emails to candidates, schedule interviews, and provide status

updates. This helps maintain communication with applicants throughout the hiring process.

5. **Candidate Database**: The ATS creates a database of candidate profiles, making it easy for employers to search and revisit past applicants who might be a good fit for future openings.

6. **Collaboration**: Multiple team members involved in the hiring process can collaborate within the ATS. They can leave feedback, share notes, and review candidate profiles in a centralized platform.

7. **Compliance and Reporting**: ATS software often includes features to help companies comply with hiring regulations and generate reports on their hiring activities.

Remember that ATS is widely used by medium to large companies to handle a high volume of job applications efficiently. It helps them save time and resources in the hiring process by automating repetitive tasks and enabling a more organised and structured approach to recruitment. Small companies, however, may not be able to afford these systems as such and some still sort through CVs by hand.

B. VIDEO INTERVIEWING TECHNOLOGY

Increasingly, employers are using AI technology to record videos of job seekers answering a standard set of interview questions. HireVue is one such company that offers video interviewing and recruitment automation technology. The company states that they have conducted millions of interviews, and they have the data to predict the best person for the job.

So, if you find yourself invited to an AI powered video interview, do take this seriously. These video interview assessments use AI to transcribe and analyse your recorded responses to quickly determine whether you are fit for the role.

C. CHATBOTS

Have you ever come across a pop-up screen on your computer with a message saying, "How may I help you?" More often than not, this is a chatbot.

Image by Mohamed Hassan from Pixabay.

A chatbot is a computer program designed to simulate human conversation, typically through text or voice interactions. Chatbots are powered by Artificial Intelligence (AI) and can engage in conversations with users, providing information, answering questions, performing tasks, and even offering recommendations.

Do you know that recruiters and employers are now using chatbots to contact potential employees rather than emailing or phoning them? Research carried out by Tidio came up with the following findings:

Chatbots in HR by Tidio.com:

- Career websites get 95% more leads by engaging with jobseekers through chatbots.

- For many HR departments, bots help free up more than 12,000 work hours annually.

- In 2023, as many as 75% of HR queries globally will occur through HR chatbots.

So chatbots are here to stay. These chatbots can answer any basic questions you may have about the company and even schedule meetings. They can also pre-screen candidates for the position advertised, saving employers and recruiters time and money.

You may be wondering just how they do this! They analyse the years of relevant experience required for the job opening, your interests and location and other questions that can be easily automated by the employer.

The image below shows the adoption rates for businesses in chatbot technology,

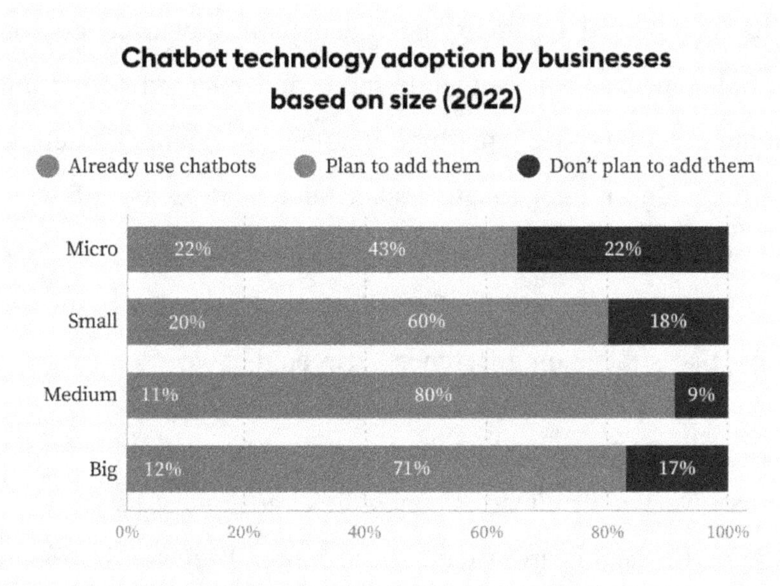

You may be thinking that chatbots have existed for many years and you would be right in this assertion. Broadly, there are two types of chatbots namely Rule-based chatbots and AI-Powered Chatbots.

Rule-based Chatbots follow a pre-configured set of rules. They churn out responses based on specific keywords and phrases which have been defined in advance. These are good for straight forward simple frequently asked questions. These are perhaps the ones you may have come across years ago.

The AI-powered Chatbots are much more advanced as you would expect. They can understand and respond to natural language. They use smarter computer programs (machine learning algorithms) to understand and make sense of what people tell them. As they interact with more users they become smarter and more capable of handling more complex enquiries. Now, that's the main difference between the two.

You will see that Chatbots have a wide range of applications across various industries, including customer service, e-commerce, healthcare, finance, and more. They can be found on websites, messaging platforms, mobile apps, and voice-activated devices.

There has been a huge uptake of Chatbots recently because they offer several benefits, such as 24/7 availability, scalability, cost savings, and the ability to handle routine and repetitive tasks; freeing up human resources for more complex and strategic work. So, remember, when applying for jobs, you could be communicating with a Chatbot who could be assessing your suitability for a position in the company. Be professional at all times.

D. CHATGPT

Many hiring professionals use ChatGPT in the recruitment process, especially small and medium sized businesses that cannot afford expensive AI tools. ChatGPT is the artificial intelligence chatbot developed by OpenAI, no doubt you may have heard of it. It launched in November 2022, and is known as the most sophisticated chatbot currently on the market, certainly the next-generation conversational AI. Below, you will see examples of questions posed by employers to get answers from ChatGPT. We call these questions 'prompts.'

Employers use it to:

1. **Write job advertisements.**

    <u>ChatGPT prompt</u>: *"Act as a recruiter. Write an advert for the position of Website Developer with WordPress expertise. Must live in Manchester and have least 2 years' experience."*

2. **Write keywords for a job description.**

    <u>ChatGPT prompt</u>: *Act like a researcher. Give me a list of keywords for the following job description. I would like to use the key words for find the right candidate. Please include any additional keywords that may not be in the job description. The job description is:*

3. **Write candidate outreach copy.**

    This is an email to send to prospective candidates telling them about a job vacancy.

    <u>ChatGPT prompt</u>: *"Here is a job description. Please write an email to try to engage new candidates, so that they become interested in applying for the job. Start with by showing that you are interested in their career progression and then present the opportunity. Outline the benefits we offer and use a convincing but friendly tone. It should be no longer than 200 words. Add a call to action and a sense of urgency."*

4. **Create an interview question bank for vacant positions.**

    <u>ChatGPT prompt</u>: *"Give me a list of 10 questions for my interview with a Digital Marketing Manager."*

5. **Create search strings to be used on other job platforms.**

   ChatGPT prompt: '*Create a Boolean search string for LinkedIn to identify an HR manager with experience in the finance sector. The HR manager should be based in London or Greater London.*" (N.B A Boolean search string is a search tool that combines keywords or an exact phrase to find specific information. Recruiters can use it to find resumes and candidates that most closely match the required qualifications).

6. **Write rejection emails.**

   ChatGPT prompt: "*Act as an experienced HR professional. Write a rejection email to John Doe, thanking him for his interest in the Media position. Use an empathetic tone and tell him we wish him the very best in his search for a job.*"

7. **Conduct recruitment market research.**

   ChatGPT prompt: "*Act as a recruitment specialist with 15+ years experience and give us some insights into the UK job market in 2023. Highlight the current trends and concerns.*"

8. Write the best job titles

<u>ChatGPT prompt</u>: *"Act as a recruiter with 10 years experience. From this (job title) and (job description) suggest the best job title I could use in a job advertisement to get the most job applications."*

This chapter has shown you how employers are using AI in the recruitment process. So, it begs the questions, shouldn't you be using AI too? Employers and other hiring professionals, recognise that AI can streamline the recruitment process, reduce bias and identify the best candidates for the job.

For you, it will also streamline your job search and have you working smarter not harder.

CHAPTER 8

AI TIPS FOR NETWORKING ON JOB BOARDS

"Registering on job portals is not just a step; it's your key to countless opportunities waiting to be discovered."

AI for Networking on Job Boards

Here is a list of the best job boards in the UK as compiled by wikihow.co.uk. This list is not ranked, they are simply the best job seeking platforms.

THE BEST 10 UK JOB BOARDS IN 2023		
1.	**Indeed**	The most popular with 10 jobs added every second.
2.	**LinkedIn Jobs**	A social network for all job seeking and professional situations.
3.	**Totaljobs**	Helps with strengthening your skills by giving useful advice. Used by thousands of small recruiters.
4.	**Reed**	Excellent for those looking for jobs in specific companies. Search for jobs by location, sectors etc.
5.	**Monster**	Best website for those who prefer to use social media to find jobs and for international jobs.

6.	**CV Library**	For those who don't have the time to scan through many jobs.
7.	**Guardian Jobs**	For those looking for high calibre jobs in specific sectors.
8.	**Adzuna**	Sends jobs only to those candidates most likely to be qualified for the position.
9.	**Glassdoor**	Good for knowing more about the company and their employees who write reviews on this job board.
10.	**WorkinStartups**	For those wanting jobs in UK startups.

Do remember to complete your profile and upload your CV on all job boards and include the all-important keywords.

In making a decision on which job sites to use, do your research to find out if they cover the type of jobs, you are looking for. Don't ignore local job sites and the more niche websites as these may serve you better.

How Can I Use AI to Create my Profile on LinkedIn?

Firstly, I will explain what LinkedIn is for the benefit of anyone who may not know about this platform. I can recollect a statement someone made online which said, *"If you are not on LinkedIn, you do not exist."*

LinkedIn is the world's largest professional network on the internet. You can use LinkedIn to find the right job or internship, connect and strengthen professional relationships, and learn the skills you need to succeed in your career. It can be found at www.linkedin.com and offers a free basic membership to anyone who wants to create and maintain a professional profile online.

You may know that LinkedIn works like a search engine for jobs. Platforms like Indeed, Glass Door, Totaljobs and Reed all use AI to match candidates with jobs. As such it is imperative that as a job seeker you complete your profile on LinkedIn and all other job platforms which include relevant keywords. By doing this, the AI tool employed will recognise your profile and give you personalised job recommendations based on your interest and skillset. Your LinkedIn profile is your career future!

ChatGPT, is a great generative AI platform to assist you in creating or updating your LinkedIn profile. I asked it the following question and here is the response it gave.

<u>ChatGPT prompt</u>: *I am new to LinkedIn. Please give me some tips to assist me in completing my profile for the first time.*

<u>ChatGPT response:</u>

Certainly! Completing your LinkedIn profile is an important step to make a strong professional impression. Here are some prompts to guide you through the process:

1. **Profile Photo**: Upload a professional photo of yourself. It should be a clear, high-quality image where you appear approachable and dressed for your industry.

2. **Headline**: Your headline is like your online business card. It's the first thing people see. Consider using your current job title and a brief description of what you do. For example: "Software Engineer | AI Enthusiast."

3. **Summary**: In your summary, introduce yourself. Share a bit about your professional background, your passions, and what you hope to achieve on LinkedIn. What are your career goals?

4. **Experience**: List your relevant work experiences. Include your job title, company, dates of employment, and a brief description of your role and responsibilities. Use action words to highlight your achievements.

5. **Education**: Add your educational background, including degrees, schools, and graduation years. You can also include academic achievements or extracurricular activities if they are relevant.

6. **Skills**: List your skills and areas of expertise. You can select from LinkedIn's predefined skill list or add your own. Try to include both technical and soft skills.

7. **Connections**: Start connecting with colleagues, friends, and other professionals you know. Networking is a significant part of LinkedIn.

8. **Recommendations**: Request recommendations from colleagues or supervisors. These endorsements can strengthen your profile's credibility.

9. **Accomplishments**: Highlight any certifications, awards, or projects you've worked on. LinkedIn provides dedicated sections for these.

10. **Volunteer Experience**: If you've volunteered, don't forget to add it. It shows your commitment to your community and can be a conversation starter.

11. **Contact Information**: Make sure your contact details are up to date. This allows potential employers or collaborators to reach out to you.

12. **Customise Your URL**: Edit your LinkedIn profile URL to make it more personalized. A simple format like "linkedin.com/in/yourname" works well.

13. **Privacy Settings**: Review your privacy settings and adjust them to your preferences. This helps you control who can see your profile and updates.

14. **Interests and Following**: Follow relevant companies, influencers, and groups in your industry. Engage with their content to stay informed.

15. **Engage and Share**: Don't just be a passive observer. Share articles, comment on posts, and engage in conversations to build your presence.

Completing your LinkedIn profile is an ongoing process, and it's a great way to establish your professional online presence. Keep it updated and stay active in the LinkedIn community to maximise its effectiveness.

I am sure that you will agree that this is a pretty comprehensive list, all generated by AI. It buttresses the importance of using AI in your job search.

This book has been written to help job seekers find a job. As such I will include a link from LinkedIn.com which featured examples of LinkedIn Profile Summaries they love. I think you will find them interesting.

14 LinkedIn Profile Summaries That We Love (And How to Boost Your Own)

https://www.linkedin.com/business/talent/blog/product-tips/linkedin-profile-summaries-that-we-love-and-how-to-boost-your-own

ChatGPT Networking and Relationship Prompts

We've looked at setting up your profile in Linkedin. Let's now look at how to network and build relationships. Networking is an essential part of the job search process. Here are some ChatGPT prompts that can help you with networking and building relationships:

1. "How can I craft an effective LinkedIn profile that attracts potential employers and connections?"

2. "What are some strategies for finding and connecting with professionals in my industry on LinkedIn?"

3. "I'm attending a networking event. Can you provide tips on how to start and maintain conversations with new contacts?"

4. "How can I request an informational interview with someone in my desired field without coming across as too pushy?"

5. "What's the best way to follow up with a new contact after a networking event or informational interview?"

6. "Can you suggest some ways to join and engage in relevant online forums or communities in my industry?"

7. "I'm interested in mentorship. How can I approach a potential mentor and build a mutually beneficial relationship?"

8. "How can I leverage my existing connections to help me find job opportunities or gain insights about the job market?"

9. "What are some strategies for networking effectively at industry conferences or trade shows?"

10. "I want to send a networking email. Can you help me craft a compelling and respectful message?"

11. "Can you provide advice on using social media, such as Twitter or Instagram, for professional networking?"

12. "I'm considering attending local networking events. How can I find relevant events in my area?"

13. "What are some best practices for maintaining long-term professional relationships and staying in touch with contacts?"

14. "Can you help me create an 'elevator pitch' for networking events to introduce myself effectively?"

15. "I'm looking to give back to my network. How can I offer help and support to others in my professional community?"

These prompts can guide you in networking effectively, whether it's through online platforms like LinkedIn, in-person events, informational interviews, or mentorship relationships. Building a strong professional network is a valuable asset in your job search and career development.

"In order to succeed, you need to take control of your Internet identity and truly present yourself in a way that inspires, impresses, and builds confidence in your abilities, products, and services. Your LinkedIn profile is the perfect tool to shape your online image." https://www.linkedin-makeover.com

CHAPTER 9

AI TOOLS FOR COVER LETTER PRODUCTION

"Cover letters are not just words, they are your personal handshake with opportunity."

AI Tools for Cover Letters

You will need to write a great cover letter if you want to stand out and be noticed during your job hunt. Having to write one for each position can be extremely time-consuming. Here's a list of AI tools that can help you wrote a cover letter.

NAME	BRIEF INFORMATION	
Resume Genius www.resumegenius.com	It starts by asking you a few questions, creates the letter and then and allows you to preview the letter.	
Zety www.zety.ai	This has lots of cover letter templates and generates a fully formatted letter.	
Live Career www.livecareer.co.uk	A simple tool that generates a complete cover letter based on your specifications.	
Kickresume www.kickresume.com	Allows you to edit the cover letter by adding your own text.	

Cover Letter Now www.cover-letter- now.com	Has several attractive templates and you can see your letter as you make it.	

ChatGPT Cover Letter Prompts

Here are some ChatGPT prompts that can help you write a compelling cover letter for a job:

1. "Can you help me craft an engaging opening paragraph for my cover letter that captures the recruiter's attention?"

2. "What are some tips for addressing the cover letter to the hiring manager if I don't know their name?"

3. "I'd like to convey my passion for the industry and the company in my cover letter. How can I do that effectively?"

4. "What should I include in the body of the cover letter to highlight my skills, experiences, and qualifications?"

5. "Can you suggest a few specific examples or achievements I can mention in my cover letter to showcase my suitability for the role?"

6. "How do I explain a career gap or change in my cover letter while still presenting myself as a strong candidate?"

7. "I want to express my enthusiasm for the company's mission. Can you help me write a convincing paragraph about that?"

8. "What are some effective ways to demonstrate that I've researched the company and understand its values and culture?"

9. "Can you provide a strong closing statement for my cover letter that encourages the reader to take action?"

10. "I'm looking for guidance on keeping my cover letter concise and to the point. What should I prioritise and what should I omit?"

11. "What's the best way to sign off a cover letter professionally?"

12. "I'd like to request an interview in my cover letter. How can I do that in a compelling manner?"

13. "How can I ensure my cover letter complements my resume and doesn't repeat the same information?"

14.   "Can you help me proofread and edit my cover letter for grammar and clarity?"

15.   "I want to make my cover letter unique. Can you suggest creative ways to stand out without being overly informal?"

Feel free to use these prompts to assist you in crafting a cover letter that effectively communicates your qualifications and enthusiasm for the job.

Cover Letter Personalised Prompts

1. *I need to write a cover letter for a __________ position. I have ___ years of experience in ___ and ___and have led a team of <u>developers</u> in my previous job.*

2. *Can you help me draft a cover letter for a <u>marketing manager</u> role? I have a strong background in <u>digital marketing</u> and have successfully led <u>multiple campaigns.</u>*

3. *I'm applying for a <u>sales executive</u> position. Could you assist in creating a cover letter that emphasises my excellent communication skills and successful sales record?*

4. *Help me write a cover letter for a <u>project manager</u> role. I want to highlight my experience in <u>managing cross-functional teams and successful project deliveries.</u>*

5. *I'm applying for a job in the <u>non-profit</u> sector. Can you guide me in writing a cover letter that shows my passion for <u>social work</u>?*

6. *I'm a recent graduate applying for an entry-level data analyst position. Can you help me draft a cover letter that focuses on my academic projects related to data analysis?*

CHAPTER 10

AI TOOLS FOR AUTO FILLING JOB APPLICATIONS

"Auto filling job applications is the shortcut to a smoother career journey."

Auto-Filling Job Applications Using AI

Ready to make your job applications a breeze? In this chapter, we will dive into the world of AI tools that make filling out those job forms feel like a walk in the park. I always say, "In the middle of all the hustle, we find ways to make things a bit easier."

So, let's see how these smart tools can bring a touch of simplicity to sharing your work story. It's not just about filling in blanks; it's about using tech to make your career journey smoother. Ready to explore with me? Let's make those job applications a piece of cake!

NAME	BRIEF INFORMATION	
JobWizard www.jobwizard.ai	This auto fills application information and gives recommendations for application answers.	
Simplify www.simplify.jobs	Completely free and uses a chrome extension to autofill job applications in one click.	

LiveCareer www.livecareer.com	A free universal tool that allows you to autofill information on several job boards like LinkedIn, Monster, Indeed, Glassdoor etc.	
Teal www.tealhq.com	A one-stop shop for auto filling job applications across 50 job boards. Autofill job applications in one click. The basic plan is free.	

How to Get a Job Using AI

CHAPTER 11

AI TOOLS FOR JOB INTERVIEW PREPARATION

"Preparing for job interviews is not just a task; it's your rehearsal for success."

AI Tools for Interview Preparation

Imagine having your own AI-powered interview coach! Do you know that there are interview preparation tools fuelled by AI, where you can step into a simulated job interview right from the comfort of your space?

These incredible tools don't just stop there – they go the extra mile by providing valuable feedback on not just what you say but also how you express it, from your responses to your body language. It's like having a virtual practice ground where you can fine-tune your interview skills, receiving guidance on where you shine and where you can improve.

I would suggest that you engage with these tools, not only to refine your interview skills but also build up that much-needed confidence to face real interviews with poise and assurance. The future of interview preparation is here, and it is personalised, empowering and ready to help you shine in your professional journey.

If you find yourself struggling to prepare interviews you may wish to utilise AI as a research tool. Choose the tool you are most comfortable with and use it regularly and for a few weeks in advance of the interview. Ask others for feedback also.

NAME	BRIEF INFORMATION	
Interviewing.io www.interviewing.io	Provides job seekers with simulated technical interviews.	
Mockmate www.mockmate.com	Allows you to practice common interview questions	
ChatGPT www.chat.openai.com	Simulates the style of an actual interview and provides feedback on your answers.	
My Interview Practice www.myinterviewpractice.com	Similar features to ChatGPT and good for practicing interview skills without any pressure.	
LinkedIn www.linkedin.com	AI-powered instant feedback tool that analyses speech content and patterns to help you test and refine your interview skills.	

Job Interview Prompts

Should prefer not to use the AI tools described above, ChatGPT is always there to help. Here are some ChatGPT prompts that can assist you in preparing for job interviews:

1. "Can you provide some common interview questions and tips on how to answer them effectively?"

2. "I have an interview for a [specific job role] position. Can you give me insights on what skills and qualifications are often emphasised in these interviews?"

3. "What are some strategies for addressing the 'Tell me about yourself' question in a job interview?"

4. "How can I prepare concise and compelling 'elevator pitches' for myself and my professional experience?"

5. "I want to showcase my problem-solving abilities in the interview. Can you provide examples of questions that might test this skill?"

6. "What are the best practices for answering behavioural interview questions, such as 'Tell me about a time when...'?"

7. "How should I discuss my strengths and weaknesses during the interview without coming across as too boastful or negative?"

8. "Can you help me create a list of questions to ask the interviewer to demonstrate my genuine interest in the company and the role?"

9. "What should I do to prepare for a virtual or remote job interview?"

10. "I'm nervous about the interview process. Can you offer some relaxation techniques and confidence-building strategies?"

11. "How can I research the company and its culture to effectively answer questions about why I want to work there?"

12. "Can you provide some guidance on professional dress code and grooming for interviews?"

13. "I'm expecting technical questions in my interview. What are some ways to prepare for and answer these questions confidently?"

14. "I want to leave a lasting impression after the interview. What can I do to follow up and express my continued interest in the position?"

15. "Can you assist me in a mock interview session to practice my responses and receive feedback?"

These prompts can help you prepare for a job interview, from understanding common questions to tailoring your responses, researching the company, and ensuring you leave a positive impression. You can use ChatGPT to practice your answers, receive tips, and build your confidence for the interview process.

Personalised Job Interview Prompts

1. Can you help me answer "Why do you want this job?" for a _____________ position?

2. How should I respond to "Where do you see yourself in five years?" for a __________ role?

3. Can you provide a response for "Describe a challenging work situation and how you overcame it" for a __________ position?

4. I need a response for "What are your greatest strengths?" for a __________ role.

5. Can you help me answer "Why did you leave your last job?" for a __________ position?

6. How can I answer, "What is your leadership style?" for a __________ role?

Courtesy of aihabit.com

CHAPTER 12

AI FOR CAREER COACHING

"Career coaching is the compass that turns professional aspirations into reality, guiding you through the maze of choices."

AI for Career Coaching.

This chapter is all about the ways Artificial Intelligence (AI) can be your personal career coach. You might be wondering, "How can a computer be a coach?" Well, get ready to be amazed!

Think of AI as your career helper, like a friendly guide that knows a lot about jobs and wants to help you find the perfect fit. It's like having a career expert right at your fingertips, 24/7.

So, what can AI do as your career coach? Let me break it down for you:

1. **Job Matchmaking Magic:** AI can sift through heaps of job information super quickly. It looks at your skills, interests, and what you enjoy doing. Then, it suggests jobs that match you like a puzzle piece finding its place.

   Example: Let's say you love drawing and have a knack for problem-solving. AI might recommend creative jobs in design or even roles that involve figuring out tricky challenges, like a puzzle solver extraordinaire!

2. **Career Path Clarity:** Ever felt lost about what career path to choose? AI can analyse your interests, strengths,

and suggest career paths that align with what makes you tick.

Example: Suppose you enjoy helping others and have a knack for organising things. AI might point you toward careers in event planning or even community organizing where your skills can shine.

3. **Learning Ally:** Want to learn new skills to level up your career game? AI can recommend courses and training to help you grow and stay ahead in your field.

   Example: Imagine you're in marketing and want to learn about social media trends. AI can suggest online courses or articles to keep you in the loop.

So, remember AI isn't just a bunch of techy words; it's your friendly career coach, here to make your job-hunting adventure smoother and more exciting than ever!

In an AI career coach platform, AI becomes the coach and individuals only engage with AI. You may find that there will be no interaction with a person or there could be very limited human interaction.

There are other types of AI coaching, which includes the hybrid model, whereby the coach utilises the information it gleans from the AI platform to provide a coaching service.

AI Tool for Career Coaching

WEBSITE	BRIEF INFORMATION	
Brain Manager www.brainmanager.co.uk	Offers a professional career test to learn what job is right for you. It will offer 10 jobs to match your personality.	

Here's a screenshot of a career test you could take now with brainmanager.co.uk. A small fee of £1.95 is charged to obtain the results.

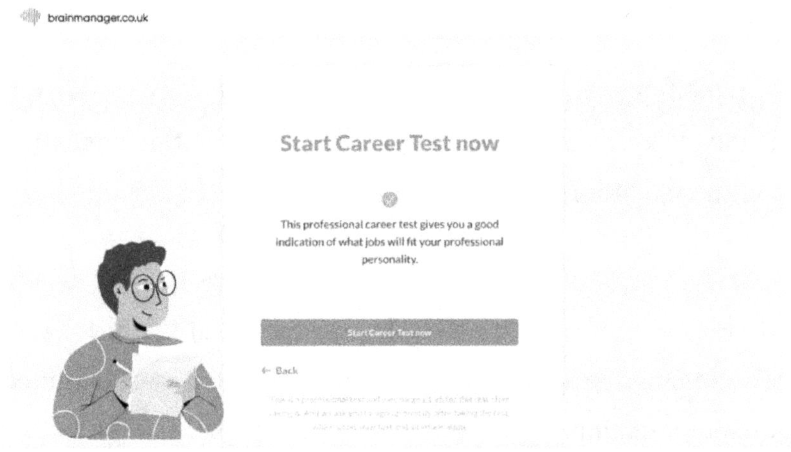

CHAPTER 13

HOW TO ENSURE JOB SECURITY IN THE AGE OF AI

"Job security in the age of AI is not about resisting change; it's about embracing innovation."

How to Ensure Job Security in the Age of AI

There is a widespread fear of job losses following the adoption of AI. The response one often gets when the topic of AI is discussed, has often been one of scepticism and trepidation at what is to come, or I should really say 'what has come'; as AI is here to stay.

While there is some element of truth in the fact that some jobs will become obsolete, many more jobs will be created, and AI cannot and will not replace all jobs because it does have limitations which we will look at in the next chapter.

It is worth mentioning that while employers see the vast benefits of adopting AI, it is seen as assisting rather than replacing jobs done by people as revealed in Microsoft's Work Trend Index.

There are several factors that could affect the longevity of your role, as we transition into AI-powered work places.

1. Flexibility and Adaptability

Are you flexible and do you adapt to new AI technology being implemented in business processes within your company? Do you feel that new AI tools would overwhelm you and/or assist you? Are you able to regulate your emotions in the workplace?

You are more likely to retain your job if you:

- Show an eagerness to learn.
- Adopt a change mindset.

- Act on adopting and testing a solution if it eliminates time-consuming tasks.

  If you are at risk of losing your job, look out for potential job opportunities and be ready to undergo training and upskilling. Most importantly be ready to leverage and collaborate with AI.

2. Intellectual Curiosity

Are you likely to want to ban or limit the development of AI technology within your organisation? Do you have questions about fairness and validity?

You are more likely to secure your job if you:

- Ask the right questions.

- Carefully evaluate the outputs of any decision.

- Reach out to colleagues with opposing opinions.

- Listen to others carefully.

3. Emotional Intelligence

Are you in control of your feelings? Are you aware of the importance of working together as a team and with your peers?

Emotional intelligence is like having a special skill to understand and manage feelings. It helps you recognise your own emotions and how they affect others, making it easier to get along with people and handle tough situations.

You are more likely to be valued in your job if you:

- Have a high level of emotional intelligence.

- Find a balance between judgement and emotional intelligence.

- Try to put yourself in the shoes of others.

- Try to focus on win-win solutions rather than winning the argument.

These three suggestions should help you develop a keen interest in keeping up with technological advancements in AI and encourage you to use it to its full potential. It is vital that you adopt a culture of lifelong learning to eliminate the fear that your job will be replaced by AI.

CHAPTER 14

HOW TO USE CHATGPT AND AI PROMPTS EFFECTIVELY

---

*"Prompt Engineering is the art
of communicating eloquently to an AI."*
Greg Brockman

Alternatives to ChatGPT

Interestingly, I read an article on BBC.com which discussed the reservations employers have about using ChatGPT in the workplace. Some employers have actually banned its use, although employees have often found a workaround to keep a step ahead. Such is the interest in using AI at work, that employees go to any lengths to gain access to this technology. Here are some alternative platforms.

ChatGPT ALTERNATIVES	
Google Bard AI www.bard.google.com	Bard uses real-time data, so it has the latest information from the internet unlike ChatGPT which has data up to 2021.
Microsoft Bing AI www.bing.com	A powerful research tool that is integrated with a web browser.
Jasper Chat www.jasperchat.ai	Jasper's AI engine pulls up-to-date information and data straight from Google. It is built for business in areas like sales, marketing and more.

Perplexity www.perplexity.ai	This features real-time information with a list of sources that can easily be verified.
Chatsonic AI www.writesonic.ai	This provides in-depth summaries and insights about ongoing news, trends and conversations. Can be used daily without any hitches.

There are others like **Best AI, Claude AI, Pi AI** and **GitHub Copilot**.

In the next section, we will explore additional prompts generated from ChatGPT to help with job applications. (Remember that prompts are simply 'questions' that you pose to the AI chat platform to generate your required response.) The prompts are:

How to use ChatGPT in Job Applications?

In an earlier chapter, I introduced ChatGPT which can be accessed by typing https://chat.openai.com/ into your web browser. The ChatGPT 3.5 version is free while ChatGPT version 4.0 requires a monthly subscription of $20.

I would strongly recommend leveraging ChatGPT as part of your job application process because it can provide valuable insights and suggestions which you may not have thought of. You may wonder, "If we all were to use ChatGPT, surely, we would all end with the same responses?"

Well, the key to getting the best out of ChatGPT and its unique content, is to provide detailed and specific prompts. The more context you provide, the better the output will be.

Before I go into more detail on how to use ChatGPT, I would like you to be aware of some key points, users are often oblivious to.

Important Points to Note When Using ChatGPT

1. ChatGPT is restricted by the training data it has learned which only goes up to January 2022. It is therefore not up to date. As such, it will not be able to provide the most accurate information at all times. If you ask ChatGPT who won the World Cup in 2022, it will not give you an answer.

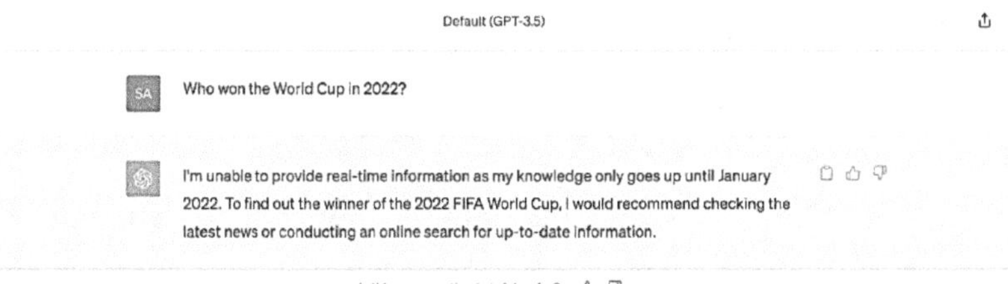

2. Double-check the information churned out by ChatGPT. Do not believe everything it says.

3. The information you input into ChatGPT is not 100% confidential. Even though it uses encryption to protect your conversations, there is always the risk that your chat could be intercepted or hacked by a malicious third party. This could lead to unauthorised access of your personal and financial information. Always remember that employees working behind the scenes at OpenAI, the founding company, could see your data even though they are required to sign confidentiality agreements.

4. You can delete all your previous conversations, by clicking on your account name at the bottom of the sidebar and selecting **Clear conversations'**. Alternatively, select **Settings**, under **General**, click the **Clear** button next to Clear all chats.

5. Safeguard your data and do not release personal information to ChatGPT.

Now, let's look at some tips on writing effective ChatGPT prompts.

Tips on Writing ChatGPT Prompts

1. Your prompt should be clear and easy to understand.

2. Specify exactly what you want. If you want a certain number of words, a number of points, a specific format, then include that in your prompt.

3. Use "Act like a" at the start of each prompt. This will improve the quality of the answer you receive. e.g. Act like an expert. Act like a teacher. Act like an employer. Etc.

4. Use examples if necessary. This will help bring some clarity to the answers you are presented with. Remember that you can train ChatGPT to produce answers in your tone or writing style.

5. Do not ask too many questions in one prompt. Focus on getting answers for one question or task first.

6. Ask ChatGPT to expand or shorten its answers depending on what you want. Continue to revise the prompts until you get the desired response.

Use the 'Regenerate' button for different variations of answers presented and choose your preferred answer.

CHAPTER 15

CONCLUSION

"Your dream job doesn't just find you; you have to chase it with passion and persistence."

Conclusion

As we reach the end of this book, I want to emphasise that your journey to landing your dream job using AI is just beginning. We've covered the ins and outs of how artificial intelligence can revolutionise your job search, and you've gained valuable insights into harnessing its power to your advantage. Now, it's time to take these lessons and put them into practice.

Remember that every step you take, every skill you acquire, and every connection you make in the world of AI and job hunting brings you closer to your goals. In a world that's constantly evolving, where AI is reshaping industries and career landscapes, your adaptability and knowledge are your most valuable assets.

As you move forward, keep these key takeaways in mind:

1. **Embrace Continuous Learning**: The journey to a successful career doesn't have an endpoint. Embrace a mindset of continuous learning. AI is evolving, and so should you.

2. **Seek Opportunities**: Actively look for opportunities to apply your AI-driven skills and insights. Stay curious and innovative in your approach.

3. **Network and Collaborate**: Remember that AI is a tool to enhance, not replace, human potential. Network with like-minded professionals, collaborate on projects, and demonstrate how humans and machines can work in harmony.

4. **Stay Resilient**: The job market can be challenging, but your newfound knowledge of AI gives you an edge. Don't be discouraged by setbacks. Instead, use them as stepping stones to future success.

5. **Be Your Best Advocate**: No one knows your skills, strengths, and aspirations better than you do. Be your own best advocate in your job search and career development.

"While you embrace new technologies, continue to grow your professional expertise and skills to ensure you stand out from the competition."

Greg Brockman

In closing, I want to leave you with one final thought: The future is bright, and AI is a tool that can amplify your potential and open doors to exciting opportunities. Use this knowledge to your advantage, stay committed to your journey, and be a trailblazer in the era of AI-powered job searches.

Your dream job is within reach, and you're well-equipped to seize it. Your future is waiting, and I can't wait to see the incredible success you'll achieve. Best of luck in your career, and may your path be filled with remarkable achievements.

Thank you for embarking on this journey with me and remember that the world of AI is yours to conquer. Your story begins now.

"Where innovation meets aspiration, opportunity is boundless."

Sandra Ramsay-Nicol

Thank you for purchasing my book. As you know reviews are the lifeblood of any author's work, so please kindly spare a moment to leave me a review on Amazon.

As a way of showing my appreciation, I would like to give you some freebies. Simply email me: booksbysandraRN@gmail.com (the RN is only in capital letters, so you don't leave it out)

FREE RESOURCES FOR ALL READERS

Email me now for:

A free copy of my eBook **"Smart Mums Don't Ignore AI"** published in 2023.

A free copy of quality prompts I would recommend for:

FREE Prompt 101:

My Career Development prompt – this is a must have!

FREE Prompt 102:

My Personal Brand prompts – showing how to build your personal brand.

FREE Prompt 103:

Negotiating and Job Offers prompts – will help you negotiate your salary.

* 9 7 8 3 6 9 1 7 4 3 8 9 0 *